ENVIRONMENTAL FOOTPRINTS

How big is your energy footprint?

Paul Mason

MACMILLAN LIBRARY

First published in 2008 by
MACMILLAN EDUCATION AUSTRALIA PTY LTD
15–19 Claremont Street, South Yarra 3141

Visit our website at www.macmillan.com.au or go directly to www.macmillanlibrary.com.au

Associated companies and representatives throughout the world.

National Library of Australia
Cataloguing-in-Publication data

Mason, Paul, 1967– .
How big is your energy footprint?

Includes index.
For primary school age.
ISBN 978 1 4202 6150 9 (hbk.).

1. Environmental degradation – Juvenile literature.
2.. Nature – Effect of human beings on – Juvenile literature.
3. Power resources – Juvenile literature. I. Title.
(Series: Mason, Paul, 1967– Environmental footprints).

304.28

Edited by Anna Fern
Text and cover design by Cristina Neri, Canary Graphic Design
Page layout by Domenic Lauricella
Photo research by Legend Images
Illustrations by Nives Porcellato and Andrew Craig

Printed in China

Acknowledgements
The author and the publisher are grateful to the following for permission to reproduce copyright material:

Front cover photograph: Earth from space © Jan Rysavy/iStockphoto; coloured footprint © Rich Harris/
iStockphoto. Images repeated throughout title.

Photos courtesy of:
AAP/AFP/Abdelhak Senna, **23**; AAP/AP Photo/Thomas Herbert, **16**; AAP Image/Solar Systems, **21**; City of
Melbourne, **27**; © Joss/Dreamstime.com, **6**; altrendo images/Getty Images, **24**; © AVTG/iStockphoto, **7**; ©
Rob Broek/iStockphoto, **13**; © william casey/iStockphoto, **19**; © Oleksandr Gumerov/iStockphoto, **8**; © Peter
Engelsted Jonasen/iStockphoto, **22**; © Magali Parise/iStockphoto, **29**; © Terraxplorer/iStockphoto, **5**; © Paul
Tessier/iStockphoto, **26**; © manuel velasco/iStockphoto, **14**; © Mark Weiss/iStockphoto, **3** (top right), **30**;
Rob Cruse Photography, **10**; © Thomas Barrat/Shutterstock, **18**; © luchschen/Shutterstock, **12**; © Losevsky
Pavel/Shutterstock, **9** (bottom); © Otmar Smit/Shutterstock, **20**; © Lee Torrens/Shutterstock, **28**; © Holger W./
Shutterstock, **11**.

While every care has been taken to trace and acknowledge copyright, the publisher tenders their apologies for any
accidental infringement where copyright has proved untraceable. Where the attempt has been unsuccessful, the
publisher welcomes information that would redress the situation.

Please note
At the time of printing, the Internet addresses appearing in this book were correct. Owing to the dynamic nature of
the Internet, however, we cannot guarantee that all these addresses will remain correct.

Contents

Glossary words
When a word is printed in **bold**, you can look up its meaning in the Glossary on page 31.

Environmental footprints

This book is about the footprints people leave behind them. But these are special footprints. They are the footprints people leave on the **environment**.

Heavy footprints

Some people leave heavy, long-lasting footprints. They do this by:

- acting in ways that harm the environment
- using up lots of **natural resources**, including water, land and energy.

It can be hundreds of years before the environment recovers from heavy footprints.

Light footprints

Other people leave light, short-lived footprints. They do this by:

- behaving in ways that harm the environment as little as possible
- using the smallest amount of natural resources they can.

The environment recovers from light footprints much more quickly.

As the world's population grows, more natural resources will be needed. It will be important not to waste resources if we are to leave light footprints.

The world's population is expected to continue growing in the future.

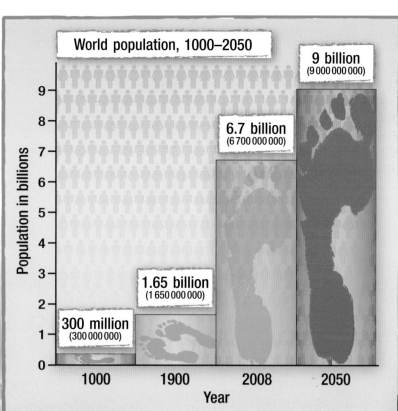

World population, 1000–2050

9 billion (9 000 000 000)

6.7 billion (6 700 000 000)

1.65 billion (1 650 000 000)

300 million (300 000 000)

Population in billions

Year

1000   1900   2008   2050

Leaving on lights in office blocks when they are not needed wastes electricity and leaves a heavy energy footprint.

What makes up an energy footprint?

An energy footprint is made up of the effects of energy use on the environment. This includes the amount of energy people use to power things such as lights, cars or televisions. It also includes the energy used to make the goods people buy, and the energy used to grow food.

A lot of energy is produced in ways that badly damage the environment. People who use a lot of this energy have heavy energy footprints. Using less energy, and energy produced in less damaging ways, leaves behind a lighter footprint.

What sort of energy footsteps are you taking? Read on to find out!

The energy industry

Energy is used to light people's homes, power their cars, grow food and make goods for people to buy. Over the last 200 years or so, a giant industry has built up around the world to provide this energy.

Where energy comes from

Traditionally, people have got most of their energy by burning things. At first, this meant burning wood for heat or light. Today, though, much of the world's energy comes from burning **fossil fuels**.

Fossil fuels include coal, petroleum oil and natural gas. People use energy from fossil fuels in various ways. They use petrol to power their cars, for example, or use electricity made by burning coal to light their homes.

Fossil fuels are burned at power stations to make the energy we need in our everyday lives.

Alternative energy sources

Alternative energy sources to fossil fuels include the Sun's energy, the power of flowing water, wind power, and the heat energy contained inside the Earth. These are all used in different parts of the world to produce energy, often in the form of electricity.

Nuclear power

Nuclear power is another alternative energy source to fossil fuels. Nuclear power is produced using **uranium**. Scientists use the uranium to produce tremendous amounts of heat, which is then used to make electricity. The world's largest reserves of uranium are in Australia, although none of Australia's energy is produced using nuclear power.

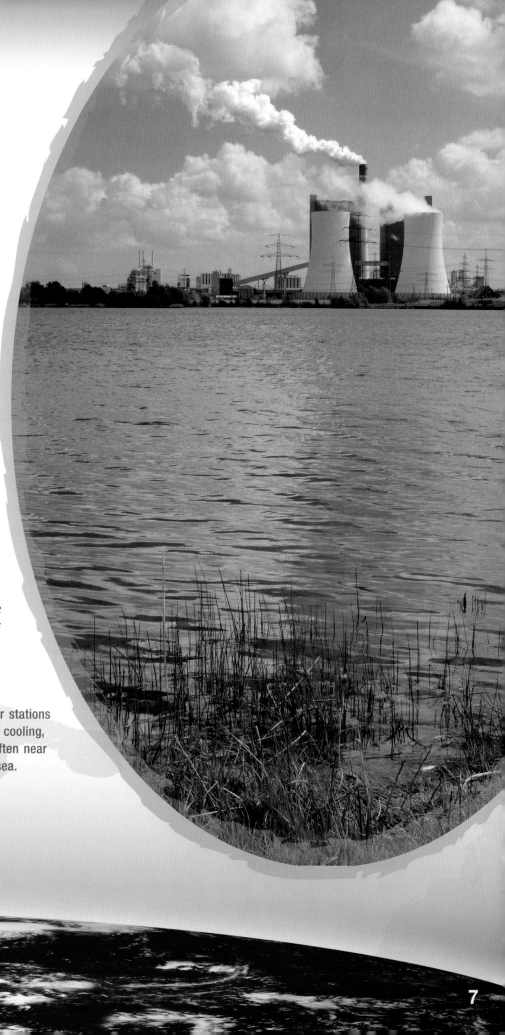

Nuclear power stations use water for cooling, so they are often near lakes or the sea.

Having plenty of energy enables us to enjoy useful appliances such as refrigerators.

Benefits of the energy industry

Many of the benefits people enjoy as part of modern daily life are a result of having affordable, plentiful energy. These benefits include:

⊕ being able to keep homes comfortably warm or cool

⊕ having light available when it is dark outside

⊕ being able to travel over long distances quickly, by car, bus, train or aeroplane

⊕ enjoying the products of modern industry, including toys, cars and computers.

Almost every aspect of our daily life depends on the energy industry.

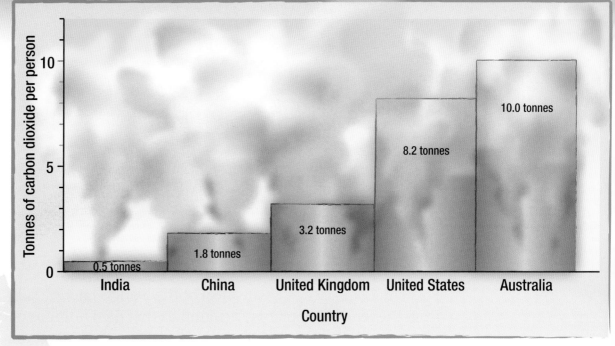

This graph shows how much carbon dioxide was released into the atmosphere per person in different countries in 2007.

Environmental costs of the energy industry

All the convenience of modern life comes with environmental costs.

- Burning large amounts of fossil fuels releases **carbon dioxide**, which has a damaging effect on the Earth's **atmosphere**.
- **Pollution** from burning fossil fuels can damage the health of living things.
- Damage to wildlife and the landscape is caused by **oil spills**.
- **Contamination** after leaks from nuclear power stations causes deaths and poisons the land for years to come.

Almost all cars release carbon dioxide pollution when their engines are running.

These costs leave behind a heavy energy footprint that will last for hundreds of years.

Energy sources

Energy sources are the raw materials from which people get energy. The type of energy sources people use affects the size of their energy footprint.

Fossil fuels

Fossil fuels are used to create most of the world's energy. They are made from the remains of plants and animals that died millions of years ago. These remains sank down under the Earth's surface. Over time, they turned into fossil fuels, either solid coal, liquid oil, or natural gas. Each of these can be burned to create usable energy.

Rethink!

Battery-powered torches and radios use up energy resources. Wind-up ones are better for the environment because they are powered by human energy.

This wind-up torch is powered by hand so it has a small energy footprint.

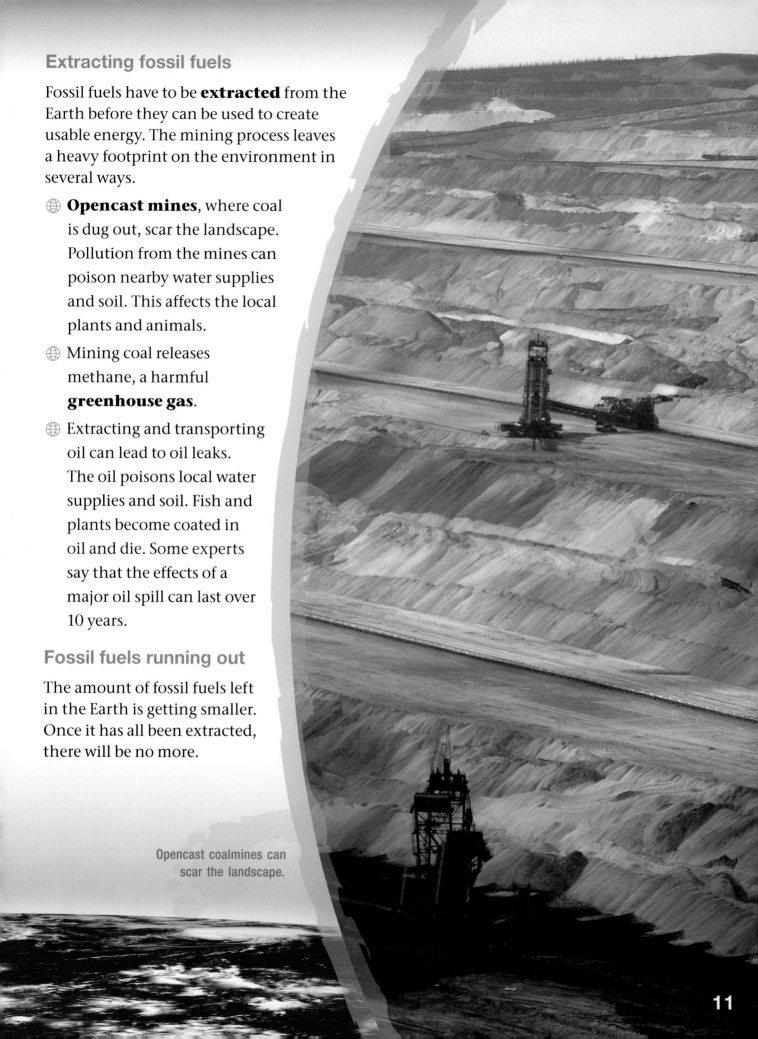

Extracting fossil fuels

Fossil fuels have to be **extracted** from the Earth before they can be used to create usable energy. The mining process leaves a heavy footprint on the environment in several ways.

- 🌐 **Opencast mines**, where coal is dug out, scar the landscape. Pollution from the mines can poison nearby water supplies and soil. This affects the local plants and animals.

- 🌐 Mining coal releases methane, a harmful **greenhouse gas**.

- 🌐 Extracting and transporting oil can lead to oil leaks. The oil poisons local water supplies and soil. Fish and plants become coated in oil and die. Some experts say that the effects of a major oil spill can last over 10 years.

Fossil fuels running out

The amount of fossil fuels left in the Earth is getting smaller. Once it has all been extracted, there will be no more.

Opencast coalmines can scar the landscape.

Clean energy sources

Clean energy sources cause little or no harm to the environment. They leave a far lighter energy footprint than fossil fuels. Many clean energy sources can be found in nature. They include the power of the wind, moving water, and the Sun.

Every day, a huge amount of solar energy falls on the Earth. Converting sunlight into usable energy makes it unnecessary to burn fossil fuels. It is also possible to get usable energy from wind, flowing rivers, waves and the Earth itself.

Solar panels provide this block of flats with electricity.

Choosing to use clean energy will give you a lighter energy footprint.

Case study

Energy from the Earth

Iceland lies over an area where there is volcanic activity close to the surface of the Earth. The people of Iceland have used heat energy from this volcanic activity since about 1930. Heat energy from the Earth is called geothermal energy.

To collect geothermal energy, pipes are drilled down into the ground and filled with water. The water heats up underground and is then pumped up to the surface. The water is then used to heat 95 per cent of city buildings and supply hot water for bathing.

Geothermal energy also provides Iceland with electricity. Heat from the Earth is used to drive **turbines**, which produce electricity. Iceland also uses the power of flowing water to make electricity. All Iceland's electrical power comes from these sources, which means Iceland has one of the lightest energy footprints of any country.

Bathers enjoy the warm water that fills lakes beside one of Iceland's many geothermal power stations.

Energy production

Producing energy damages the environment. How much it damages the environment depends on how the energy is produced. This determines how heavy the energy's footprint is.

Fossil-fuel power stations

Fossil-fuel power stations can burn oil and gas to produce electrical energy, but most burn coal. The heat produced from burning fossil fuel is used to create steam, which drives turbines. These turbines create electrical energy that can be used by homes and industries.

However, burning fossil fuels is linked to **global warming**, the biggest threat to the environment today. Global warming is the increase in the Earth's average temperature.

Rethink!

Using the standby button on electrical appliances wastes electricity. Turning them off instead reduces their energy footprint.

Using the off switch instead of standby cuts a television's energy use by about 10 per cent.

Global warming

Global warming is happening right now. As the Earth's temperatures rise, **desert** spreads, rainfall becomes less predictable and sea levels get higher as polar ice melts. The world's weather may become more extreme, with more **droughts**, **hurricanes**, floods and other disasters.

Causes of global warming

Almost all scientists agree that humans are contributing to global warming. One of the ways they are doing this is by burning fossil fuels. This releases greenhouse gases, which trap heat within the Earth's atmosphere. Fossil-fuel power stations burn huge amounts of fuel each day. The energy they produce has a heavy energy footprint.

Greenhouse gases, especially carbon dioxide, are released when fossil fuels are burned and help to increase global warming.

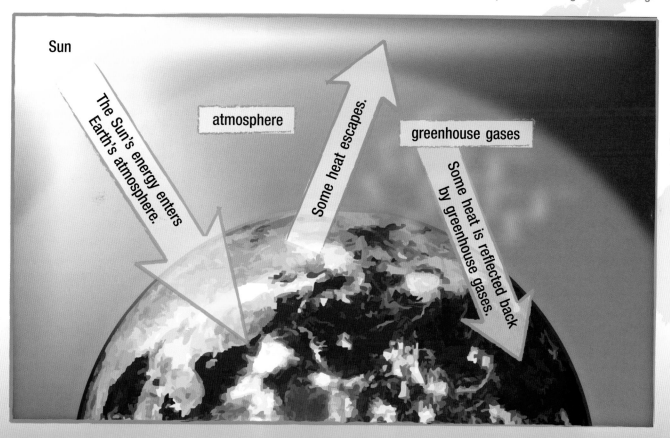

Sun

atmosphere

greenhouse gases

The Sun's energy enters Earth's atmosphere.

Some heat escapes.

Some heat is reflected back by greenhouse gases.

Nuclear power stations

Nuclear power stations are an alternative to fossil-fuel power stations because generating nuclear power does not produce greenhouse gases. Nuclear power can affect the environment in other ways, however. It can have an extremely heavy environmental footprint.

Radiation leaks

Nuclear power stations produce radiation, which is harmful to living things. Radiation is usually very carefully contained within a power station, but it sometimes leaks out. When this happens, it can affect the environment for thousands of kilometres and over many years.

Nuclear waste

Waste material from nuclear power stations releases radiation for hundreds of years. Unless this waste is sealed away, the radiation leaks out and poisons the environment.

Nuclear waste is so dangerous that it has to be transported in special containers.

Case study

Chernobyl nuclear disaster

On Saturday 26 April 1986, the world's worst nuclear disaster happened at Chernobyl in Ukraine. An explosion at the Chernobyl nuclear power plant shot **radioactive material** high into the sky, to be blown by the wind.

By Monday 28 April, the radioactive waste had spread as far away as Sweden. It would eventually spread over thousands of kilometres.

As a result of the accident:

- 🌐 large areas of land could no longer be used to grow crops or raise animals
- 🌐 rivers were poisoned
- 🌐 between 4000 and 93 000 people are eventually expected to die due to the radiation.

Between 5 and 8 million people still live in areas affected by the disaster. The long-term effects on their health are not yet known.

The Chernobyl disaster affected most of Europe.

Dose of radiation – multiples of normal rate

- No detectable rise
- .001–1
- 1–5
- 5–10
- 10–20
- 20–40
- 40–100
- 100+

Hydro-electric power

Hydro-electric power is produced by flowing water. Usually, water from a dam pours through an opening, driving a turbine. The turbine produces electricity.

Hydro-electric power does not produce greenhouse gases, but it affects the environment in other ways. When a dam is first built, for example, the land behind it is flooded. People, plants and animals lose their homes. Despite this, many people argue that hydro-electric energy has a far lighter footprint than fossil-fuel energy.

Biomass energy

Biomass energy comes from plants. The biomass is burned to provide heat, in the same way as fossil fuels are burned. Burning biomass releases the same amount of carbon dioxide that the plants removed from the atmosphere while growing.

The Three Gorges Dam hydro-electric project in China generates electricity from the power of moving water.

Rethink!

When plants grow, they take in carbon dioxide from the air. Planting trees is a good way to reduce the amount of harmful greenhouse gases in the atmosphere.

Wind turbines are often grouped together in 'wind farms'.

Power from the sea

Waves and tides wash against most of the world's coasts. Several ways to use the movement of the sea to generate electricity have been invented. In the future, this could become an important light-footprint source of energy.

Geothermal energy

Geothermal energy comes from the heat within the Earth. It can be used to produce both hot water and electricity.

Wind power

Wind power can be used to produce energy. The wind turns propellers on giant wind turbines. The turbines make electricity. No greenhouse gases are released once the turbines are built, so wind-power energy has a very light energy footprint. Around the world, twelve times as much wind-power electricity was produced in 2007 as in 1997.

Solar power

Solar power is energy that comes from the Sun. It can be used to make hot water and electricity for homes and businesses. In places where the Sun shines a lot, 'solar farms' have been set up to harvest the Sun's energy. Once the farms have been set up, they have a very light energy footprint.

Small-scale energy production

Wind and solar power can both be used to produce energy on a small scale. People can put solar panels on the roof of their house, or they can use a small wind turbine or hydro-power device to generate electricity. This gives them a very light energy footprint. In many countries, it is possible for small-scale energy producers to sell any leftover electricity to the power companies.

These solar panels will help the home owner save money on electricity bills, as well as having a light energy footprint.

Choosing to use energy whose production is less harmful to the environment, such as biomass energy, hydro-electricity, and geothermal, solar and wind power, will give you a lighter energy footprint.

Case study

Carnarvon solar-energy farm

In October 2005, a solar-energy farm opened in the town of Carnarvon, in Western Australia. Carnarvon was chosen partly because it is one of the areas in the world that gets the most energy from the Sun.

The farm started relatively small, with just 144 solar panels. Even so, in its first year the farm produced enough energy to supply Carnarvon with power for four days.

It would have taken about 10 000 litres of fuel oil to produce a similar amount of energy.

Solar energy produces no greenhouse gases, so electricity from Carnarvon solar energy farm has a light energy footprint.

The solar panels at a solar energy farm are lined up so that they catch as much of the Sun's energy as possible.

Energy use

People use energy for many things in their daily lives. How they use it has a big effect on their energy footprint. Using energy when you do not need it creates a heavier footprint. Saving energy creates a lighter one.

Travel

Transport is one of the main sources of carbon dioxide, a greenhouse gas that is one of the causes of global warming. Cars, most buses, trucks and aeroplanes get their energy by burning fossil fuels. Trains run on electricity which is also usually produced by burning fossil fuels.

Rethink!

Travelling on foot or by bicycle instead of in a car reduces the size of people's energy footprints.

Special lanes for cyclists to use make it safer to travel by bike.

Case study
Carbon offsetting

Carbon offsetting is a way for people to try to make up for the carbon dioxide gas released by burning fossil fuels. It first became popular as a way of making up for travelling by aeroplane, which burns large amounts of fossil fuel.

Carbon offsetting works by planting trees, because trees use carbon dioxide to grow. The original idea was that paying for trees to be planted would use up the carbon dioxide that had been released.

Today, carbon-offset organisations offer other ways to make up for carbon dioxide pollution such as:

- buying solar panels for people in poorer countries, so that they will not need to burn fossil fuels for light
- paying for small hydro-electric power stations to be built in poorer countries, so that electricity will not have to come from burning fossil fuels.

These offer alternative ways to fill in the energy footprint left behind by burning fossil fuels.

Solar panels installed on this house in Morocco through a carbon-offsetting scheme produce enough electricity to power four to eight light bulbs.

Energy at home

In wealthy countries, energy used at home produces a quarter of the carbon dioxide that is released by energy use. Saving energy at home can make a person's energy footprint much lighter.

Heating and cooling

Controlling the temperature inside homes uses up a lot of energy. Boilers usually burn gas to heat water for radiators. Putting on extra clothing instead of turning up the heater saves energy and results in a lighter footprint.

Air conditioning for cooling runs on electricity. Wearing loose, cool clothes and using cold drinks to cool down instead of having the air conditioner on saves energy.

Turning down the temperature control on the heating and putting on a warm pullover saves a lot of energy.

Case study
Ground-source heat pumps

Ground-source heat pumps are an alternative to heating and cooling systems that use fossil fuels. Not far below the Earth's surface, the ground stays at a steady temperature. This enables ground-source heat pumps to warm or cool buildings.

A pipe is sunk down into the ground. Water is pumped through the pipe and back to the surface.

If the building above is cold, the water is warm in comparison and warms the building up. If the building is hotter than the ground, the water carries some of this heat underground, where it is **absorbed**.

If the water is pumped through the system using solar or hydro-electric energy, ground-source heat pumps have a very light energy footprint.

Heating and cooling a house with a ground-source heat pump produces a lot less carbon dioxide than other heating and cooling systems that use fossil fuels.

cool water

warm water

Light bulbs

Light bulbs run on electricity. They only use small amounts, but lots of small amounts add up. Many people today use low-energy light bulbs and make sure they turn off lights in rooms that are not being used.

Electronic devices

Electronic devices use electrical energy. The more devices people use, the heavier their energy footprints. It is possible to save energy by:

- unplugging devices such as stereos, televisions and computers when they are not being used
- never using the standby button
- only using devices such as washing machines, dishwashers and tumble dryers when they are full.

Saving energy in these ways will lighten your energy footprint.

Houses that use low-energy light bulbs reduce their power bills and have smaller energy footprints.

Choosing to take simple steps to use less energy in your everyday life will give you a lighter energy footprint.

Case study
Council House 2

Council House 2, also known as CH_2, in Melbourne, is Australia's most environmentally friendly office building. It is filled with features designed to lighten CH_2's energy footprint.

- The computer screens need only 50 per cent as much energy as normal.
- Low-energy lights use only 35 per cent as much energy as normal.
- The north side is shielded from the Sun's heat by a 'vertical garden' of vines.
- Inside, CH_2 is heated or cooled using the Sun's energy, water, and wind turbines.
- Sixty per cent of the building's hot water comes from solar panels on the roof.

CH_2 is far better for the environment than the office building it replaced. It uses 15 per cent of the electricity, 13 per cent of the gas and 28 per cent of the water used by the previous building. It also produces only 13 per cent of the greenhouse gases.

CH_2 is a ten-storey office building in Melbourne, Australia.

How big is your energy footprint?

The size of a person's energy footprint depends on how the energy they use was made, and how much they use. How big do you think your footprint is?

Where does your energy come from?

Energy from sources that do little or no harm to the environment has a light footprint. Producing light-footprint energy does not release greenhouse gases into the atmosphere. Solar energy, wind energy, water power and geothermal energy are all 'clean' energy sources.

Nuclear energy produces no carbon dioxide, but there are major safety concerns about nuclear accidents and nuclear waste.

Burning fossil fuels to release their energy releases greenhouse gases. These are the main cause of global warming. Using energy from fossil fuels makes your energy footprint heavier.

How big do you think your energy footprint is?

Wind power is a source of 'clean' energy.

Rethink!

Electricity companies now supply at least some of their energy from green energy sources. This is produced in ways that are less harmful to the environment.

Work out your energy footprint!

Ask yourself how often ('never', 'sometimes' or 'often') you do these things:

- 🌐 travel by bicycle or walk
- 🌐 travel by ship or train rather than by aeroplane
- 🌐 have a cold drink instead of turning on the air conditioning
- 🌐 get up to turn off the television or stereo instead of using standby
- 🌐 turn off the computer instead of letting it sleep.

Walking or riding a bike are easy ways to reduce your energy footprint.

If your answers are mostly 'never', you have a heavy energy footprint. If you mostly answered 'sometimes', your footprints are average. If you gave a lot of 'often' answers, you are leaving only light environmental footprints.

future energy footprints

You can choose to take light footsteps or heavy footsteps. If people continue leaving heavy footprints, it could affect the environment for thousands of years to come.

What you can do

The Internet is a great way to find out more about what you can do to take lighter footsteps. Try visiting these websites:

⊕ **www.wikihow.com/Reduce-Your-Greenhouse-Gas-Emissions**
This site contains lots of advice on how to reduce the size of your greenhouse-gas footprint.

⊕ **www.wikihow.com/Buy-a-Carbon-Offset**
Here you can find out how to buy a worthwhile carbon offset to fill in your environmental footprint from using a lot of fossil-fuel energy.

⊕ **www.elementree.com.au/calculator.asp**
This site has a carbon calculator, where you can work out how big your environmental footprint is at home, through motor travel and through air travel.

Some of the search terms you might use to find information about energy and the environment include:

⊕ coal-fired power stations, pollution

⊕ geothermal energy, Iceland and New Zealand

⊕ energy, carbon calculator.

What will YOU do to change your energy footprint in the future?

Glossary

absorbed
soaked up or taken in

atmosphere
the layer of gases that surrounds the Earth, enabling humans, animals, plants and other creatures to survive

carbon dioxide
a gas that is used by plants to help them grow, and which is released when fossil fuels are burned

contamination
making something impure or dirty by introducing harmful or poisonous material

desert
area with very little water, where only very specialised plants and animals can live

droughts
periods of time without enough rainfall, when water becomes scarce, crops fail, and plants and animals suffer or die

environment
the natural world, including plants, animals, land, rivers and seas

extracted
taken out or removed

fossil fuels
the remains of plants and animals from millions of years ago, which have been buried deep under the Earth's surface and there turned into coal, oil and gas

global warming
process by which the Earth's average temperature is getting warmer

greenhouse gas
gas that contributes to global warming which is often released when fossil fuels are burned

hurricanes
violent storms with very high winds, capable of damaging buildings, trees and other things

natural resources
natural substances, such as wood, metal, coal or water, which can be used by humans

oil spills
accidental leaks of petroleum oil into the natural environment

opencast mines
giant pits dug at the surface of the ground in order to get out coal or other minerals

pollution
damaging substances, especially chemicals or waste products, that harm the environment

radioactive material
a substance that releases a stream of tiny particles which, in all but the smallest doses, are poisonous to most living things

solar power
power from the Sun, which can be turned into electricity by solar panels

turbines
machines in which moving fluid or gas, such as water or steam, rushes through and forces propeller blades to spin, which can be used to make electricity

uranium
a poisonous mineral that affects the health of plants and animals when it breaks down

Index